The Adventures of Harry the Rhode Island Boat Dog

Lynn Hile Hughes

Publisher's Information

EBookBakery Books

Author contact: lynnhughes401@gmail.com

Website: lynnhilehughes.wordpress.com

ISBN 978-1-953080-57-8

Dedication

To Harry the Dog ....

... with thanks to Kate Hughes, Edward Hughes and I. Michael Grossman for their invaluable help and to Terry Jeremiah for her help and role as Harry's #1 fan.

Coast
Daylight

Waters I Sailed with My Pack

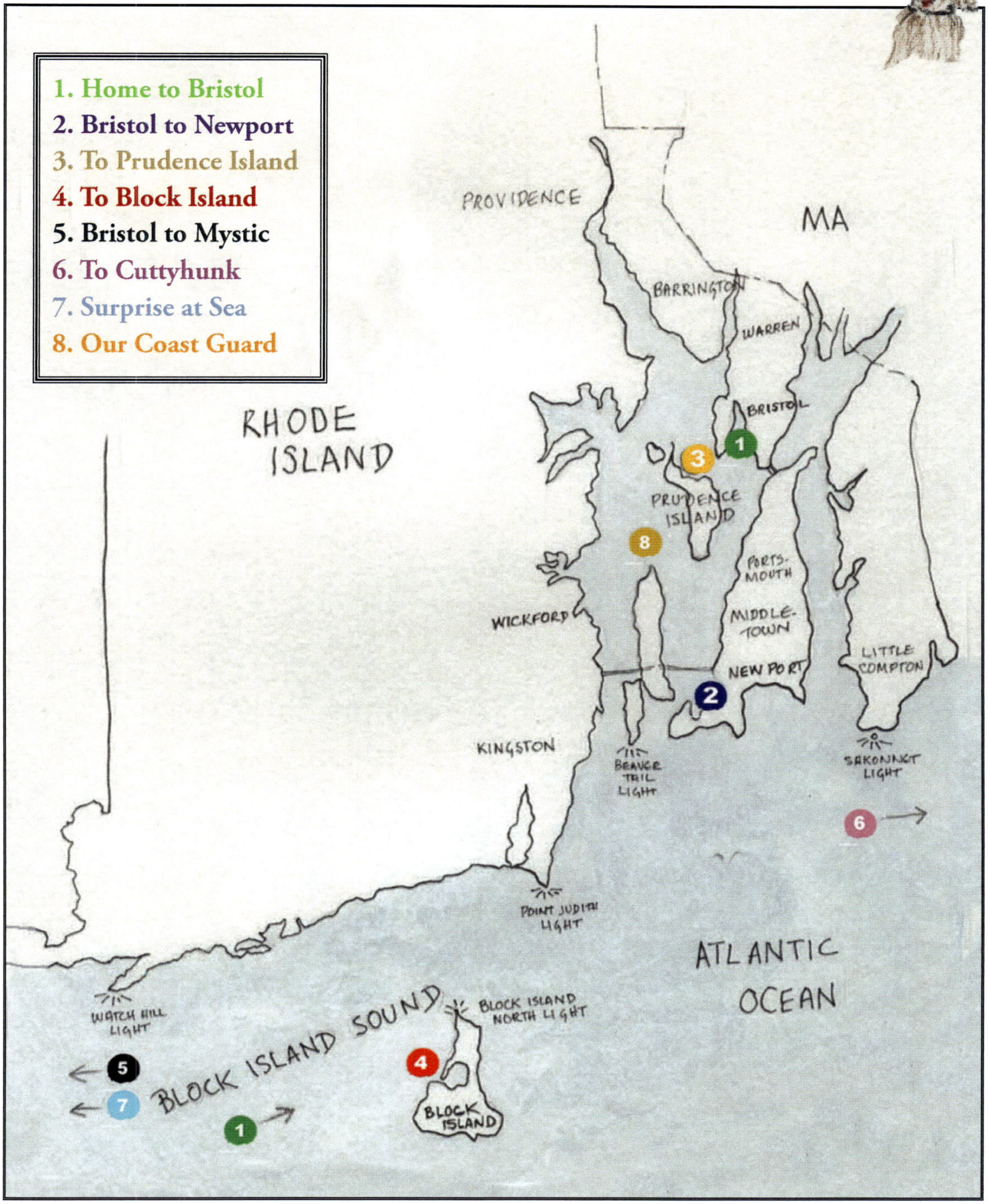

All About Me

Hi! I'm Harry, a medium-sized Wheaten terrier mix and was just 8 months old when I adopted Lynn and Bob on July 14, 2012 from the Medfield Animal Shelter in Massachusetts.

I was ready to start some adventures! They talked about buying a boat. Would adopting them and their boat make ME a Rhode Island Boat Dog? Is there a test? Is it hard?

They were nice and I liked them (and I needed a home), so we all got in the car and drove, with me in the back seat, to my new home in Rhode Island on the East Bay. That's where the Warren River joins Narragansett Bay, near Jacob's Point Marsh.

And, I Get a Life Preserver

First, I was fitted with a doggy life preserver – a little one – because I was still a puppy. My pack wasn't sure I could swim.

It turned out I didn't like to swim. Water is much too wet and usually very cold. I will walk in the water, but not if it is too deep and as long as my pack is on the other side (preferably with a treat).

So, on the boat, a life preserver at all times!

1

Long Island to Bristol

We Bring Our New Boat Home

Our first trip was to bring our new boat back from South Jamesport, on the North Fork of Long Island, to our harbor in Bristol, Rhode Island. My pack was new to motorboating, but not to sailing, so we set off on a sunny, windy day in April.

Once we got out of the shelter of land it was...

WHOOOOEEE!

Wind! Waves!

Water splashing everywhere!

Waves were breaking over the bow of the boat and onto the windshield.

Yikes!!

I curled up inside the cabin. Too much water flying around for me!

Bob and I Take Command

After 10 minutes of that scary-ness, we made a U-turn and almost immediately the water calmed down.

Much better!

Once we got into the shelter of the North Fork, I was on the flying bridge directing Bob into the first marina in Greenport.

No wind and waves here.

We Travel Long Island Sound

Two weeks later, with wind, waves and tides going with us, we had a lovely trip across Long Island Sound, past Block Island.

Who knew that motorboats had to worry about wind and tide? Now I know, because I'm learning to be a Rhode Island Boat Dog.

I Learn My First Boating Lesson

Lesson 1 *on being a Rhode Island Boat Dog:*
In rough weather trawlers (and our motorboat was a trawler) don't like wind, waves and tide opposing each other. So take yourself to a quiet, comfortable out of the way spot and stay there!

Block Island North Light

How Do We Get to Shore?

We arrived at our new home port of Bristol Harbor and picked up our assigned mooring ball. The ball was connected to a sea anchor to hold our boat in place in the harbor. But the shore was pretty far away from our boat. So how would we get to land? We were told that the answer was to call *Olivia* on the walkie-talkie.

Who is *Olivia*, anyway?

And how would she get us to shore?

Could she carry all of us at one time?

Would we get wet?

And, what's a walkie-talkie?

Olivia Isn't a Person...
She's A Launch!

Olivia was a boat! Smaller than *Coast Daylight* (by a lot), and properly called a launch.

She (boats are called "she") is made to carry people, packages and gear from the land to and from their boats.

That's why Olivia has lots of seats for passengers and places for storing bags and gear.

I Meet Mike and Kelly

Mike, one of *Olivia's* drivers and chief in charge of things, welcomed us to Bristol. He became a BFF. We loved him, and he always had kind words to say to me.

So we hopped down into *Olivia* and were ferried to the dock in Bristol.

Kelly, who was our other favorite driver, and I got along so well that we also became BFFs. Kelly had three-year-old twins, and sometimes they came on *Olivia* to help her drive the boat.

That was the most fun! We were all about the same size and loved to point our noses into the wind. *Yes!*

I Learn Even More About Boats

Until I became a Rhode Island Boat Dog, I had no idea that boats had their own language, but now I know.

I made a list of boat things and what we really call them when we're not on the boat. The list is called a *Glossary*, and it's at the end of this book.

Lesson 2 *on being a Rhode Island Boat Dog: Learn what the words in the Glossary mean.*

2

Off to Newport

We Motor South Past Mt. Hope Bridge

We started exploring Narragansett Bay with a trip to Newport. We loaded up bags of lunch, drinks and sweaters and called good friends to join us for an adventure. I put on my life preserver; we all piled into *Olivia*, the launch, and Kelly took us out to Coast Daylight on her mooring in Bristol Harbor.

We all stepped up onto *Coast Daylight's* deck (well, I was lifted by the handle of my life jacket). We opened the doors and windows, took off the canvas covers, started the diesel engine, and let go of the mooring.

Coast Daylight motored south out of Bristol Harbor and Hog Island, past Mt. Hope Bridge.

Hog Island Light

And... past Prudence Island and its Little Lighthouse...

...And finally past the Naval War College, under the Jamestown Bridge and past Rose Island Light.

So Much To See!

Lots of little Optimist sailboats greeted us at the entrance to Newport Harbor, right next to Fort Adams. That's right – a real Fort guarding the harbor.

Fort Adams was built in 1799 to protect Newport, first during the War of 1812, and then in other wars.

Happily (through it looks so scary, or maybe it was lucky), there never was a shot fired in anger.

I like that.

A Pup Has To Eat - Especially At Sea

Time for lunch! Great! Good sandwiches that we picked up at our favorite sandwich shop, Ricotti's, and cold drinks, fruit, and cookies.

I'm on floor patrol for any dropped food and am usually the recipient of good pieces of sandwich from the crew! (I put on my most charming expression, and, if possible, rest my chin on someone's knee – the most effective for handouts).

As we munch on lunch, we enter Newport Harbor and make a full circuit, admiring all the fabulous (according to everybody on board) yachts. I think lunch was much more fabulous. After a full tour of the harbor, we went back out past Fort Adams, made a right turn, went under the Newport Bridge and then motored back to our mooring in Bristol Harbor.

Lesson 3 *on being a Rhode Island Boat Dog: Floor food is next best to being handed a piece of sandwich or a dog treat. My pack appreciates how clean I keep the decks!*

We Visit Potter's Cove (at Prudence Island)

Another trip my pack and I love on a really hot day is a trip on *Coast Daylight* over to Potter's Cove for a swim. It's only a half hour from Bristol.

We pick up our usual crew, our friends who love the boat, and our favorite sandwiches. I put on my life preserver, get aboard *Olivia* and then onto *Coast Daylight.*

The weather that day was super steamy. So, off we went, South out of Bristol Harbor, made a right turn at the end of Poppasquash Point and then headed over to Potter's Cove. There we dropped the anchor. I supervised at the bow to make sure Lynn had things under control, while Bob had the helm from the flying bridge.

Then (and all this took time) we went to the stern, lowered the dinghy (since it was in our way to get into the water) and lowered the swim ladder. **Then *WE ALL JUMPED IN!***

Well... Not All Of Us Jumped In...

I tried swimming once, and I much prefer walking and running on dry land and riding IN the boat. So, I was on guard duty while everyone else swam. That was important duty, by the way, so I patrolled by walking around the boat on the deck and counted heads to make sure everyone was OK and accounted for.

Lesson 4 *on being a Rhode Island Boat Dog: Guard the boat when no one else is on board.*

Coast
Daylight

Anchor Up and We Head Home

When we (meaning my crew) finished swimming, we reversed the entry process – got out of the water using the ladder, pulled the ladder up, rehung the dinghy, started the engine, pulled up anchor and *Vrooom!*

Off we went, back to Bristol Harbor.

Actually, *Coast Daylight* doesn't "Vroooom!" anywhere. She sips diesel fuel and travels at the stately pace of 8 knots (you and I can walk at 4 knots...) and I can run faster than that!

4

Off to Block Island!

Another favorite of ours is a trip to Block Island. It's 9 miles off the coast of Rhode Island and 24 miles from Newport and on the map it looks like a drawing of a pork chop! It takes a while to get there at eight knots – so Lynn, Bob, and I always stayed there for a few nights.

I had a surprise the first time I went to Block Island. When we arrived at Great Salt Pond, a boat that looked just like *Olivia* (at least to me) came up beside us. I decided to speed the process of getting to shore and jump into what I thought was *Olivia* without any help. Oops! Not only did I miss the deck of the *Olivia* look-alike, I missed the boat entirely ***and landed in the water!!***

I Get Rescued From My Unplanned Swim

The boat turned out not to be Olivia, but the Harbormaster collecting our overnight rent. She was very quick to fish me out and put me back on my own deck before I really had time to get very wet. Thank you, Block Island Harbormaster!

HARBOR PATROL
Coast Daylight

Lesson 5 *on being a Rhode Island Boat Dog: It is VERY IMPORTANT to know where you are stepping when you get on or off a boat.*

The other thing about Block Island and Great Salt Pond is that to go for a walk, I had to go for a dinghy ride to shore. And then another dinghy ride back to *Coast Daylight*. Quite a production, but a nice mini sea voyage.

THE OAR
GROCERIES

Cuisine to My Liking

There was also a launch at Block Island (like *Olivia*, but not exactly) that we could call on the walkie-talkie to come over to our boat. We'd step aboard and get dropped off at the dock next to The Oar restaurant. Easy!

...And another (very good) thing about Block Island is Aldo! Every morning (very early) Aldo fills his boat at the dock with bread, pastries, egg muffins (a personal favorite), coffee and tea from his bakery on the island, and he motors out into Great Salt Pond where all the boats are moored. Then he calls out, *Aldo, Aldo!*

Andiamo! Every morning! You wave to him and he drives his boat over to your boat, asks you what you would like for breakfast, and there it is. No muss. No fuss. He even takes credit cards!

Let's Go To Mystic

Between Us, I'm Partial to Mystic

For our next Big Trip my pack decided to go to one of their favorite places, Mystic Seaport. We could stay overnight at the dock, walk around the Seaport after it closed and have dinner at a local restaurant.

Fun!

And we pass through two drawbridges to get to the Seaport from Fisher's Island Sound!

So, we left Bristol Harbor early in the morning on a lovely sunny day and made our way down the West Passage of Narragansett Bay to Point Judith Lighthouse. From there we headed for Block Island Sound.

Point Judith Light

Drawbridges are Just Plain Thrilling

We all sat up on the flying bridge, and there was still a good breeze to blow my ears back.

It took a whole day to get to Mystic by sea while it would have taken just over an hour by car. But speed, as we know, is not the point of going by boat!

Since we'd be living on *Coast Daylight* for four days, we brought not only our lunch, but also food for other meals. *Coast Daylight* has a nice galley, with a refrigerator, sink with hot and cold water, a stove and even an oven.

After a few hours traveling along the coast of Rhode Island, we passed Watch Hill Light and entered Fisher's Island Sound. From there we turned right at the Mystic River – and ahead of us were two drawbridges, one for Amtrak trains and the second for the cars on the road through the town of Mystic.

We called the Amtrak Bridge Tender and asked when we could pass through the drawbridge. The Bridge Tender replied that the bridge would open after the next

Eastbound train passed over the bridge and we could safely pass then (which we did). The Amtrak Bridge is a swing bridge. It swings away from the waiting boats to let them through.

Next was the Mystic River Road Bridge and that opens at 15 minutes before the hour and 15 minutes after the hour. We called the Bridge Tender and asked that we be allowed through at the next opening. This bridge is a bascule. There is a huge weight on the side of the roadway over the river, and when the weight is released by the Bridge Tender, the weight goes down and the bridge goes up. Very different from the Railroad Bridge.

The Bridge Tenders Give Us Permission to Pass

In the distance you can see the beautiful, quiet harbor.

Here we are going through the road bridge. I was sitting on the bow and got a hearty wave from the Bridge Tender!

Once through that drawbridge, instantly, we were in the beautiful quiet harbor, surrounded by historic buildings, sailboats, motor boats and a schooner, the *L.A. Dunton* and the whaling ship, *Charles W. Morgan.*

Lesson 6 *on being a Rhode Island Boat Dog: Always check with the Bridge Tender before you go through the bridge.*

My Personal V-Berth for Sleeping at Sea

We called the Mystic Dockmaster for instructions on where to dock *Coast Daylight*. With her help we tied up to the pier next to the Seaport. It was a great spot with lots to see – people, buildings, boats.

We got off the boat and took a nice long walk around the Seaport. Then dinner for me. Next up – guard dog duty for me (also known as an after-dinner nap) while Lynn and Bob went out for dinner. Then another walk. The Seaport village closes every night, and the only people left are the boaters at the Mystic dock.

It's so much fun to explore Mystic Seaport when no one else is there! It's like a quiet little village with everybody asleep. Speaking of which, time for bed!

You may wonder where we sleep on *Coast Daylight*. During the day I sleep on the settee by the dining table or on someone's lap, but at night it's cozier in the V-berth in the cabin in the bow of the boat. There is a second cabin aft with a nice big bed, windows with venetian blinds and, just like the cabin in the front, it has its own head with a shower. The aft head even has a tiny bathtub!

We Head Home After Our Mystic Adventure

After a day and another night at the dock at Mystic, we left (very early) to catch the opening of the Mystic River Road Bridge, traveled back through the railroad drawbridge, made a left into Fisher's Island Sound, passed through the Race, past Watch Hill Light and got back home to Bristol Harbor in the late afternoon.

6

Off to Cuttyhunk!

Just South of the coast of Massachusetts lie the Elizabeth Islands. There are 20 islands, mostly uninhabited, but Cuttyhunk has a population of 52, according to *Wikipedia*. It is the first island you come to on the right after passing Sakonnet Light at the very Southern tip of Rhode Island.

Cuttyhunk is very small, has no cars, but has a lovely protected harbor, some small shops (dinghy in, dinghy out, no launch) and flourishing oyster beds. Every evening, about 5pm, the seafood boat brings clams, oysters and shrimp cocktail to the visiting boats moored in the harbor.

You order just what you want. They open the clams and oysters right there in front of you, make up the plates and pass them to you in your boat. Then your crew passes over some money to pay for the treats and settles down with their fresh seafood to watch the sun set and eat dinner.

It's a fabulous place for swimming (If you care to). I watch and make sure everyone's head is visible above the water! It is also just a wonderful place to spend a few days (or weeks).

7

A Surprise on Long Island Sound

We took another big trip down to New York, and to our old home port of Sutton Manor in New Rochelle to visit our friends. We stayed in the New Rochelle Marina and had a wonderful time.

On the way back, we stopped for the night at the marina in Stratford, Connecticut and another night in Mystic (outside the drawbridges this time, but close to the Chicken Little restaurant, which has the most WONDERFUL breakfast).

The weather on Long Island Sound was beautiful, not too hot, wind from the right direction. We had an early start from Stratford, down the Housatonic River and then a left (East) into Long Island Sound.

Lynn and Bob took turns steering and our ride was uneventful... UNTIL! We saw a plume of water shoot straight up in the air. In the middle of nowhere. *Wait! What was that?*

We slowed down. There it was again. A plume of water plus a large dark shadow. And again, a few minutes later, another plume of water, a large dark shadow AND a smaller dark shadow.

Binoculars in hand, my pack watched that patch of water. This time they both shouted "It's a whale!" and "There's a baby whale too!"

We turned the engine off quickly and sat silently watching the whale show. And a whale show it was. A humpback mother whale was diving and resurfacing with her calf following.

Another boat joined us, also with the motor off. We all sat watching the whales play for at least an hour.

Lesson 7 *on being a Rhode Island Boat Dog: Be on the lookout whenever you're on the boat. It may not be as fun and exciting as our own whale show, but it may prevent hitting floating debris or avoiding an upcoming storm.*

8

Boarding

The last exciting adventure I will share with you is the day we were boarded by the Coast Guard.

We were returning from Newport home to Bristol on a quiet weekday afternoon. Off in the distance we spotted one of the Coast Guard boats that not only patrol the Bay, but, in fact, all the water next to the United States. The Coast Guard regulates and inspects vessels and maritime facilities, conducting safety checks to reduce the risk of maritime pollution. They are the police of the coastal waters. Usually, the Coast Guard boats pass by us with a wave, but this time they came right over to us and announced that we were being boarded for an inspection.

Yikes! They tied their boat alongside ours. First, they asked if the dog was dangerous. The dog?

Me? Dangerous?

No Ma'am, No Sir. (Unless you try and take away my stuffed bear). Then they asked if we had weapons aboard.

No Sir, No Ma'am.

Then two of the Coast Guard officers came aboard, while two maintained watch on their boat. They checked our fire extinguishers, driver's licenses, (but not my dog license tag on my collar), the paperwork about the boat, our heads and through hull fittings. Then they wrote up their visit and gave us a copy.

We passed their tests. *Phew.*

After they left, we felt very well taken care of and happy that we, and our boat, had passed inspection (and that I wasn't dangerous).

The only thing missing was a biscuit from the officers for the dog on guard duty (me).

Lesson 8 *on being a Rhode Island Boat Dog: If you meet the Coast Guard, thank them for keeping us all safe!*

And that, my good friends, is all the adventures that this book has room for. If you should see me on the boat, please wave...

...or on the East Bay Bike Path, please give me a High Five!

Glossary

(In order of use)

Chapter One:

In the lea – out of the wind, in shelter

Bow – the front of the boat

Gunwhale (pronounced gunnel) – the top edge of the hull on a boat (on *Coast Daylight* the railing sits on top of it)

Walkie-Talkie – phone for boaters to call each other (and the shore)

Launch – boats that carry people, packages and gear from land to boats and boats to land

Chapter Two:

Mooring – an anchor attached to a float, like a ball, that holds the boat in place

Optimist (*Opti*) – a small sailboat (about the size of a bath tub), usually used to teach children to sail but also for adults - especially for winter frostbiting races

Chapter Three:

Helm – where the boat's steering wheel is located (or tiller, if the boat doesn't have a wheel)

Flying Bridge – the very topmost level of the boat. *Coast Daylight* had another steering wheel and controls up there, just like the ones in the main cabin

Stern – back of the boat

Dinghy – a little boat carried aboard a bigger boat to get to the shore and back. It is either rowed or has a small engine (it can also have a sail and then it's a sailing dinghy)

Chapter Four:

Harbormaster (no separate name for a woman in the job) – like police for the harbor

Chapter Five:

Galley – boat kitchen

Bridge Tender – the operator of a draw bridge, or swing bridge, or railroad bridge

Settee – a couch on a boat, fixed to the wall and floor

V-berth – two beds in the cabin in the bow of the boat put together so they form the letter "V"

Head – bathroom
Aft – back of the boat

Chapter Six:

Shuck – what opening an oyster or a clam is called. The Shucker does all the work with a shucking knife.

Checklist of What it Takes If You Want to Become An Official Rhode Island Boat Dog

[✓] **Lesson 1**: Trawlers don't like wind, waves and tide opposing each other, so find a quiet place to settle down and take a nap. Do not walk around on the deck!

[✓] **Lesson 2:** Learn what each word in the Glossary means.

[✓] **Lesson 3:** Floor food is next best to being handed a piece of sandwich or a dog treat. A Rhode Island Boat dog has to keep the decks clean at all times!

[✓] **Lesson 4:** It's a dog's duty to guard the boat when no one else is on board.

[✓] **Lesson 5:** It is VERY IMPORTANT to know where you are stepping when you get on or off a boat.

[✓] **Lesson 6:** Always check with the Bridge Tender before you go through a bridge.

[✓] **Lesson 7:** Be on the lookout whenever you're on the boat.

[✓] **Lesson 8:** Thank your Coast Guard for keeping us safe.

If you can check of all of the above items as I did, and learn all the lessons by heart, you have passed the test and are an Official Rhode Island Boat Dog! *Congratulations! Dog biscuits all around!*

Your Official Rhode Island Boat Dog Certificate follows on the next page. Cut on the dotted line, ask your pack to fill in your name and then hang it proudly over your dog bed.

OFFICIAL RHODE ISLAND BOAT DOG CERTIFICATE

Awarded to:

____

Date

____

Official Signature
Harry the Rhode Island Boat Dog

About Lynn

by Harry the Dog

So, enough about me. Lynn and her husband Bob sailed on Long Island Sound and took a yearly trip to Narragansett Bay from their home in New Rochelle. Once they retired, it was to Rhode Island. They moved from a sailboat to a trawler. I agreed with their choice: comfier bunks and softer seats.

Kate and Edward are their children, and I love them! They take me for walks and feed me treats! Sometimes they try to take me for runs, but I know better.

They also have dogs - there is Rusty, the red fox Labrador (who I've only met on FaceTime because he lives very far away). He is VERY BIG. And then there are the Doober girls, Gracie and Pepper Potato.

That's Rusty on the left then the Doober girls, Gracie and Pepper. They're Havanese and very little. Gracie, Pepper and I hang out together pretty often since they live nearby. They are really funny, and we have a great time running around like noodle brains!

OK, back to Lynn.

She has always loved to draw - houses, lighthouses, flowers, boats and dogs. She retired from banking and finance and had more time to draw, so she started a series of East Bay Bike Path Weeds (aka Wildflowers). Then we went on the boat, and she could draw all the active lighthouses in Rhode Island. Her latest series is native Rhode Island birds.

Meet Harry's Neighborhood Friends in Lynn's first book,

The Bagy Bunch Solves A Mystery

The Bagy Bunch has a mystery to solve! Strange footprints have appeared. Who do they belong to? Can you help the bunch solve the mystery?

Made in the USA
Coppell, TX
09 June 2026

80013013R00043